PROVERBS

A STRONG MAN IS WISE

PROVERBS

A STRONG MAN IS WISE

A 30-DAY DEVOTIONAL

VINCE MILLER

PROVERBS
Published by David C Cook
4050 Lee Vance Drive
Colorado Springs, CO 80918 U.S.A.

Integrity Music Limited, a Division of David C Cook
Brighton, East Sussex BN1 2RE, England

The website addresses recommended throughout this book are offered as a
resource to you. These websites are not intended in any way to be or imply an
endorsement on the part of David C Cook, nor do we vouch for their content.

Library of Congress Control Number 2023934905
ISBN 978-0-8307-8622-0
eISBN 978-0-8307-8625-1

The Team: Luke McKinnon, Jeff Gerke, Jack Campbell, Karen Sherry
Cover Design: James Hershberger

Printed in the United States of America
First Edition 2023

1 2 3 4 5 6 7 8 9 10

050923

CONTENTS

Contents

To my three amazing children: Faith, Grant, and Riley. Thank you for challenging me to be a godly father. I thought of you daily while writing each of these devotionals. I pray they will be a reminder to you of me and my convictions about the Bible, Jesus, the Spirit, and God our Father. You are my daughter and sons, but even more, you are my sister and brothers in Christ. I love you. Dad.

ABOUT VINCE MILLER

Vince Miller was born in Vallejo, California, and grew up on the West Coast. At twenty, he made a profession of faith while in college and felt a strong, sudden call to work in full-time ministry. After college and graduate school, he invested two decades working with notable ministries like Young Life and InterVarsity Christian Fellowship, as well as in the local church and in senior interim roles. He currently lives in St. Paul, Minnesota, with his wife, Christina, and their three teenage children.

In March 2014, he founded Resolute out of his passion for discipleship and leadership development of men. This passion was born out of his personal need for growth. Vince turned everywhere to find a man who would mentor, disciple, and develop him throughout his spiritual life. He often received one of two answers from well-meaning Christian leaders: *either they did not know what to do in a mentoring relationship or they simply did not have the time to do it.*

Vince soon learned that he was not alone. Many Christian men were seeking this type of mentoring relationship. Therefore, he felt compelled to build an organization that would focus on two things: ensuring that men who want to be discipled have the opportunity and giving them real tools with which to disciple other men.

Vince is known as an authentic and transparent leader who loves to communicate with men and who has a deep passion for God's Word. He has authored several books, and he is the primary creator of all Resolute content and training materials.

INTRODUCTION

Years ago, I started writing devotionals, which I shared with my children. As a father, I was trying to find ways to speak into their everyday lives. The idea was to put Scripture in front of them daily because I knew God's Word and his Son, the Living Word of God, would have a supernatural effect on their lives.

Now I'll admit that, at first, I wasn't sure they were even reading them. But I came to discover they were not only reading them, but they were also sharing them with their friends. One day, another dad found out what I was doing, and he suggested sending the devotionals to other fathers to share with their families as well. That turned into the *Men's Daily Devo*, which over one hundred thousand men read, listen to, or watch every day (found at beresolute.org/mdd).

I share this because to some degree that's what's happening at the start of the book of Proverbs. A father, Solomon, is sharing wisdom with his son, and the world has been given the pleasure of listening in. Except Solomon's wisdom is far beyond mine, and his "subscriber base" is in the billions and still growing.

Who was Solomon? He was the son of David and Bathsheba, and the third and final king of the united kingdom of Israel. He came to the throne at age twenty and reigned for about forty years. He is best known for five things: building the Temple, his wealth, his wisdom, his writings, and his wives. Solomon had a lot of wives, which was a sin that led to his downfall and resulted in the divided kingdom.

But as the Bible tells us in 1 Kings 3–4, after young Solomon took his place on the throne, he asked God for one thing: wisdom. God rewarded him for asking for this, and not other things, by granting him wisdom and all the other things too. Thus, Solomon became one major source of wisdom in the ancient world. What we read in Proverbs is primarily attributed to him, even though other authors contributed—and though Solomon himself wrote and accumulated much more than is in the book.

What I love about Proverbs is that it's written by a man for men in a way that men can easily consume and apply. What we are about to read together is not just an accumulation of wisdom statements. It's also godly insight that when applied will increase our skill in living a godly life. When we finish, we will have become wiser, or more skilled, men of God. A strong man, after all, is wise.

Each day we will read a proverb that speaks to some aspect of a man's journey. I hope these daily readings will inform, challenge, and inspire you. Each devotional will conclude with a question, suggested action, and a prayer. Please take a few minutes to reflect and let the Spirit convict you. Journal your ideas in the space provided, or on your phone or in a separate notebook. You might go through this book with another brother and take a daily journey together through the book of Proverbs.

I hope you'll enjoy these devotionals as we become strong and wise together.

NEVER STOP

"Hear, my son, your father's instruction, and forsake not
your mother's teaching, for they are a graceful garland
for your head and pendants for your neck."

Proverbs 1:8–9

Most of Proverbs was written by King Solomon, son of King David, to whom God granted wisdom far beyond his years. The book of Proverbs is a collection of some of his wise sayings given as a father to a son.

I was drawn to the words quoted above because they assume something of high importance is happening in the home. They assume a father and mother are instructing and teaching. And they assume that this is happening in the home by parents who invest their time in their most important students—their children.

However, this is not so much the case anymore, is it? To a great degree, we have handed the instruction and teaching of our children over to "professional educators," who are now informing and leading our kids. This has been happening for decades. But now, I think we are seeing the consequences of this error in our judgment.

Our kids are getting educated not only by teachers who don't share our values, but also by social media, YouTube, and coaches, who spend more time with them than we do. No longer are our children learning about sex, identity, and history from us. Now they're learning about these things apart from us, away from the home, and apart from the biblical perspective. Just hoping that our kids will have a Christian teacher, coach, or friend is not a plan—because hope alone is not a plan.

But beyond parents willing to instruct, something else is needed: a son or daughter who will *listen* and *not reject* their teaching. Both are important: parents who intentionally teach, and children who intentionally listen.

> It's never too late to teach, and it's never too late to listen.

Brother, this is hard work. The hardest of all work. You know how I know? Because I have been both the belligerent son and the lazy father. And I bet you have too. The only way to make it right is to never stop listening and never stop teaching.

So if you are a father, teach your children (or grandchildren) something today. Don't overcomplicate this. Just text them your favorite Bible verse and explain why you like it. And then, if you are a son whose parents are still living, listen more carefully to your parents today. Ask them a question about how they would handle a present situation in your life, and then just listen for the wisdom.

Remember, it's never too late to teach, and it's never too late to listen. Let's redeem the wisdom of Solomon here and bring education, leadership, willingness, honor, and God back to our homes.

ASK THIS

What do you need to teach as a father? How do you need to listen better as a son?

DO THIS

Teach, listen, and don't quit.

PRAY THIS

God, give me the willingness to listen. Then give me the wisdom to teach.

JOURNAL

NEVER STOP

TALK IT OUT WITH A WISE MAN

"So you will be delivered from the forbidden woman,
from the adulteress with her smooth words, who forsakes
the companion of her youth and forgets the covenant of
her God; for her house sinks down to death, and her
paths to the departed; none who go to her come back,
nor do they regain the paths of life."

Proverbs 2:16–19

In this passage, Solomon gives his son wisdom about sexual sin. But these words can apply to anything we want. Solomon suggests that wise men can actually see the future. They can see what is forbidden before it traps them. They can see seduction before they are seduced. They can see inconsistencies before integrity is lost. And they can learn from the bad decisions of others before they make their own bad decisions.

While this is encouraging, it assumes a few things about his son. First, it assumes that his son knows right from wrong. Second, it assumes that his son is willing to take time to discern right from wrong. Third, it assumes that his son is ready to choose right over wrong.

Solomon suggests that wise men can actually see the future.

However, because we are all imperfect at this, Solomon presents his son with an intriguing discipleship process in four simple steps:

1. Do you see the consequences of this decision?
2. Do you see the seduction of this decision?
3. Do you see the inconsistencies of this decision?
4. Do you see what happened to others who made this decision?

This is precisely why we need wise men in our lives: They see things we don't. They have questions—and answers to questions—we haven't even thought about. So today, if you need good advice on the next big decision in your life or if you are about to make a decision that you really want to make—stop. Don't make that decision. Put it off for a bit. Instead, take these four questions to a godly man and talk it out.

Don't be seduced by what you want or what others want for you. Do what God wants you to do. Act right and be righteous by doing the hard work to get wisdom.

ASK THIS

What big decision are you about to make? Or what decision do you want to make that you're not sure you should make?

DO THIS

Talk it out with a wise and godly man.

PRAY THIS

God, stop me from making decisions that honor my will. Let me make decisions that honor your will.

JOURNAL
TALK IT OUT WITH A WISE MAN

DON'T REJECT DISCIPLINE

"My son, do not despise the LORD's discipline or be
weary of his reproof, for the LORD reproves him whom
he loves, as a father the son in whom he delights."

Proverbs 3:11–12

I can honestly say I despised correction during a part of my life. Correction made me feel like I was a complete failure. Therefore, I used to interpret all correction negatively. And to add to my error, I would privately demonize the people who corrected me, holding a secret grudge about what they said and how they said it.

But at some point, I'm not sure when, I started to see correction differently. I unlearned my hatred of correction and the people who corrected me. This was hard, and it took years, but I discovered that people who corrected me were really doing so for my benefit. I came to realize that this was even true of people who corrected me poorly—because some people tend to correct others very poorly, very often.

And yet, correction, which in this text is called "discipline," is something that's guaranteed to happen in a man's life. Solomon teaches his son that he should not hate discipline or the discipliner. Instead, he should push through the negative emotional impact of the discipline and see the love and benefit behind it. Solomon is giving his son advice to help him grow through emotional challenges more quickly so he can have increased benefit from discipline in his life.

This is what godly men do who experience accelerated growth. They see discipline differently. In fact, they see it three times: They see it first for the immediate corrections they need to make. They see it second for the benefit it will bring in their lives. They see it third from the perspective of the God behind it all.

> Push through the negative emotional impact of the discipline and see the love and benefit behind it.

So, if you encounter correction or discipline today, see it three times.

1. See the immediate correction you need to make.
2. See the benefits correction will provide you long term.
3. See the sovereign love of the Father for you.

And remember that your Father delights in you.

ASK THIS

Are you experiencing discipline in your life right now?
What is it?

DO THIS

Look at it three times.

PRAY THIS

God, take away my hatred of correction and discipline.

JOURNAL
DON'T REJECT DISCIPLINE

BUILD YOUR PRECEPTS

"Hear, O sons, a father's instruction, and be attentive, that you may gain insight, for I give you good precepts; do not forsake my teaching. When I was a son with my father, tender, the only one in the sight of my mother, he taught me and said to me, 'Let your heart hold fast my words; keep my commandments, and live.'"

Proverbs 4:1–4

When I first read this passage, I admit that I did so with two regrets. The first was the regret that I didn't have a father growing up who might have passed precepts on to me. The second was the regret that I didn't pass on more precepts to my children. I found myself reflecting on what my kids might remember, if anything, of the precepts that I attempted to give them.

But then I caught myself. I saw a flaw in the logic of my regret: the assumption that it was "too late" to share precepts with my children. It's not too late. Then I remembered one of those precepts that I repeat almost daily: "Live all in for him who lived all in for you."

Live all in for him who lived all in for you.

Today, spend a couple of minutes recalling those precepts or axiomatic statements you remember from your past. I am sure there is at least one that is worth passing on. While you are at it, start building your list. Write them down in a journal or on sticky notes. If you dare, share one today. Your precept might help others to build their own lists. Speak it out loud so others will know the principles that drive your life.

ASK THIS

What's a precept or axiom you want others to remember?

DO THIS

Share it one time today. Start by sharing it in the following journaling area.

PRAY THIS

God, I choose to live by your precepts and share them with others.

JOURNAL
BUILD YOUR PRECEPTS

DISCIPLINE TODAY, GREATNESS TOMORROW

"My son, be attentive to my words; incline your ear to my sayings. Let them not escape from your sight; keep them within your heart. For they are life to those who find them, and healing to all their flesh. Keep your heart with all vigilance, for from it flow the springs of life. Put away from you crooked speech, and put devious talk far from you. Let your eyes look directly forward, and your gaze be straight before you. Ponder the path of your feet; then all your ways will be sure. Do not swerve to the right or to the left; turn your foot away from evil."

Proverbs 4:20–27

Some people might fly past this section of Solomon's wisdom, assuming it's trivial. But wisdom is not trivial. Solomon understood that "trivial" matters produce significant success. He understood that simple, repetitive behaviors have the potential to produce tremendous long-term gains.

If you want to be great at something, you'll have to make a bunch of small changes and sustain them over a long period of time.

Consider the best athlete you know. Whoever that is, I guarantee that even though they are genetically gifted, they know the importance of discipline in a way that average athletes do not. They wake and sleep on a regimen. They eat primarily for calories, not taste. They carefully monitor their input and output. They train for hours each day, stretching, working, and strengthening their body. They have very specific training plans that build over months. They watch and study films of others in their sport for hours on end.

When we, the spectators, are entranced by their performance, we might think that if we owned the same gear and imitated the way they played, we would get the same results. You know what that is—it's laughable. Because the secret to their performance on gameday is the hundreds and thousands of hours of discipline over years that got them there. This is true of anybody who is an expert in their field.

Here, Solomon applies this principle to his son's character. He encourages three fundamental disciplines: First, the discipline of what he sees. Second, the discipline of what he speaks. Third, the discipline of how he walks.

These are not trivial. What we look at, what we say, and how we walk are not trivial activities. They are fundamental, and they must be disciplined. And great men discipline them consistently. They discipline all three daily—eyes, mouth, and action.

> Wisdom is not trivial. Solomon understood that "trivial" matters produce significant success.

Now, this can be overwhelming if you have never considered it. So here is your action step for today: pick one of the three—your eyes, mouth, or action—and make a covenant of discipline with it. Make it a covenant that you agree to implement daily for a long time. For example, you could choose to make a covenant to never curse with your mouth again. And then, if this is your choice, I want you to declare it by sharing it with someone. I want your word to be a covenant between you and God. Then I want you to discipline yourself daily when it comes to the language you use.

No, you are not going to be perfect in your practice right away, but that's okay. Because disciplining your mouth will take time. But if you do this daily over a long period, it has the potential to produce tremendous long-term gains. Some of these gains you will see only further down the road.

Then, let's talk in ten years or so and you can let me know how you are doing. Because somewhere right about that ten-year point, someone else will notice how disciplined you are and will want the same for themselves. Then you can share this same wisdom with them, like I did with you. And like Solomon did with his son. Be disciplined today and be great tomorrow.

ASK THIS

Which one do you need to discipline—your eyes, mouth, or action?

DO THIS

Make a covenant of discipline.

PRAY THIS

God, receive my covenant of discipline. And may the
Spirit give me strength to live it out.

REGULATE YOUR DESIRES

"My son, be attentive to my wisdom; incline your ear
to my understanding, that you may keep discretion,
and your lips may guard knowledge. For the lips of a
forbidden woman drip honey, and her speech is
smoother than oil, but in the end she is bitter as
wormwood, sharp as a two-edged sword."

Proverbs 5:1–4

Solomon is not demonizing women here. Like a good father, he is warning his son of the dangers of two sinful people: the immoral woman and the immoral man. He wants his son to know that both men and women have desires that are sometimes incredibly strong. So much so that when a man stops regulating his desires, they will act in a way they shouldn't. And while God gave these desires to men and women, he wants them to be satisfied the right way—the best way. Not by something or someone forbidden.

A man can't let his desires run wild. He must use discretion on every sweet and savory presentation he encounters. Not just the allure of the person presenting it, but the lure of the desires within himself. Because if a man cannot regulate his desires, two things will happen: First, he will discover the bitter, sharp, and deadly end of these desires. And second, he will miss out on the best satisfaction for his desires because he chose the unsavory ones.

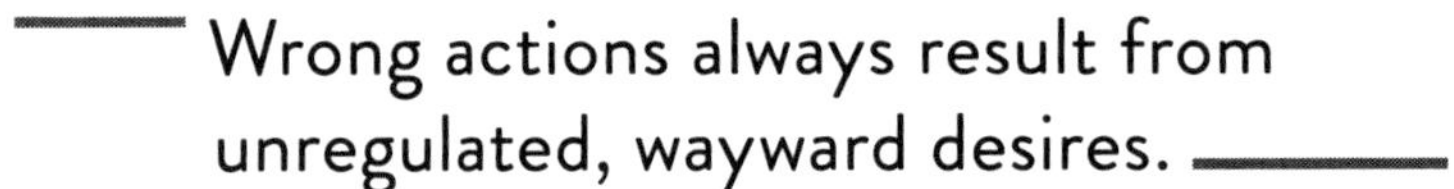

Wrong actions always result from unregulated, wayward desires.

If you are a father, I know you might get all worked up about having "the talk" with your kids. But the talk that Solomon gives here is far more strategic. It's a talk about the desires within a man and a woman. I believe this is a far more important topic, because wrong actions always result from unregulated, wayward desires. Desires that are given the freedom to run wild.

To prove this point, recall one of the most significant challenges that Jesus presented to men. It wasn't exclusively focused on action but the desires that led to the action:

> You have heard that it was said, "You shall not commit adultery." But I say to you that everyone who looks at a woman with lustful intent has already committed adultery with her in his heart. (Matt. 5:27–28)

ASK THIS

What desires do you need to regulate?

DO THIS

Take action to regulate them before they produce the wrong results.

PRAY THIS

God, show me the desires I need to regulate. And may your Spirit give me strength to regulate them when I need redirection the most.

JOURNAL
REGULATE YOUR DESIRES

LAWS THAT GOVERN MEN

"Go to the ant, O sluggard; consider her ways,
and be wise. Without having any chief, officer,
or ruler, she prepares her bread in summer and
gathers her food in harvest."

Proverbs 6:6–8

Intuitively, we all know that natural moral laws govern all mankind. There are universal moral standards that serve as the basis for how we live and do life. Most of the time, we don't pay attention to them because we assume them. We might call them "unspoken natural moral laws."

But occasionally, someone violates one of them. For example, a peer shares a secret or a partner breaks a promise. And in these moments, we think about these laws because someone has violated them. We bumped into the injustice of these unlawful violations.

In this text, Solomon is giving us a law because he wants us to avoid injustice. He imagines two simultaneous events. One is a lazy man who is doing nothing. Right next to him is a mound covered with busy ants. Solomon sees a natural law at work, one that teaches something about how to live. So here are the four lessons we learn from this one high-contrast event:

- Law One—Be a hard worker, not a slacker.
- Law Two—Be self-motivated, not constantly motivated by others.
- Law Three—Be industrious; don't wait around for someone to provide solutions.
- Law Four—Be prepared, not surprised by changing seasons.

But these natural moral laws have an even more important lesson to teach us: that we want and need to be governed. Otherwise, we will live in chaos and injustice. While we might see and adhere to natural laws in this world, not everybody will live by them. They are there for a reason—to point us to something. They point us to a Lawgiver. Someone who established the laws in the first place. And that Lawgiver is God.

> We want and need to be governed. Otherwise, we will live in chaos and injustice.

With God, other laws are at work that supersede natural laws yet don't violate them. Here are two of them: first, the law of universal sin (which says that you are sinful and live in a sinful and broken world); and second, the law of God's grace (which says that God wants to save you from your sin because you cannot save yourself).

So today, get out there and be moral. But when you see sin or you behave immorally, remember that we worship a Lawgiver who governs all things and extends grace to you and all who sin.

ASK THIS

How do you need to govern your action today? What are you learning about the Lawgiver?

DO THIS

Be lawful and worship the Lawgiver.

PRAY THIS

God, forgive me for breaking your laws. Cleanse me of immoral thoughts and behavior. Extend to me your law of grace.

JOURNAL

LAWS THAT GOVERN MEN

THE BLESSING IS IN THE WISDOM

"And now, O sons, listen to me: blessed are those who keep my ways. Hear instruction and be wise, and do not neglect it. Blessed is the one who listens to me, watching daily at my gates, waiting beside my doors. For whoever finds me finds life and obtains favor from the LORD, but he who fails to find me injures himself; all who hate me love death."

Proverbs 8:32–36

Nothing is more exciting to a teacher than an eager student, a ready disciple, a coachable player, or a willing son. Such a person has the highest potential for growth and change. They usually develop at speeds that surpass others.

But notice that this disposition is incredibly potent when combined with godly wisdom. The combination of an eager man with divine wisdom results in great blessing. It's a simple equation. But the blessing is not just in the outcomes. The blessing is the relationship with wisdom itself. There is a blessing in learning, watching, finding, waiting, and obtaining wisdom. This is where the adventure is: right in the middle of the pursuit of wisdom. Not just in the outcomes.

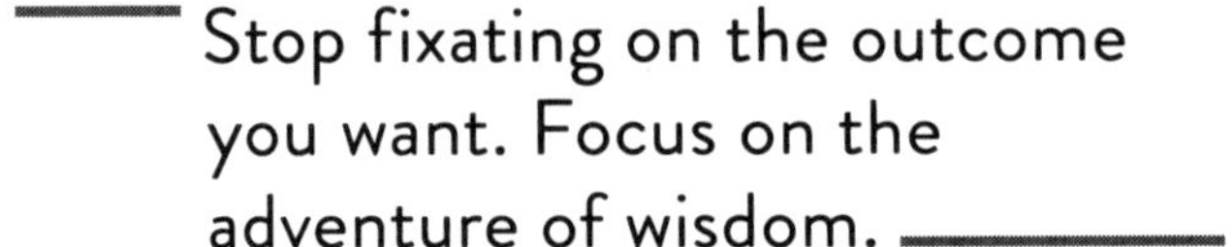

So, where in your life do you need wisdom? Name it. Say it out loud. Right now.

And then stop fixating on the outcome you want. Focus on the adventure of wisdom. Live in the moment and let wisdom do its teaching. And when the outcomes arrive, enjoy those too.

ASK THIS

Where in your life do you need wisdom?

DO THIS

Name it and say it out loud and write it out.

PRAY THIS

God, I am confused. But give me the wisdom I need in the place I just proclaimed.

JOURNAL

THE BLESSING IS IN THE WISDOM

TWO TYPES OF MEN

"Whoever corrects a scoffer gets himself abuse, and he who reproves a wicked man incurs injury. Do not reprove a scoffer, or he will hate you; reprove a wise man, and he will love you. Give instruction to a wise man, and he will be still wiser; teach a righteous man, and he will increase in learning."

Proverbs 9:7–9

Solomon informs us that there are two types of men. Type one is the man who can't (or won't) be corrected. Type two is the man who can be corrected. Type one despises you when you correct him, and he perceives you as his enemy. Type two loves you and perceives you as his friend. And thus, each man has a different response to correction: type one injures and is abusive, and type two increases in wisdom.

I think we would all love to be known as the type of men who can receive correction. But no man always receives it perfectly. This is because:

1. We don't always agree with the correction that was delivered.
2. We don't always like how the correction was delivered.

3. We don't always like the person who delivered
   the correction.

These are three big reasons. But as soon as we focus on any one of these three things, we get caught in the trap of the type-one man. We move our focus from what needs to change in us to what needs to change in others. And if we feel cornered, we will fight our way out until we have injured the people delivering correction in the way we feel injured by them.

> Rather than being defensive toward others, be on offense against the sin that lies within your own heart.

But the type-two man, the man who can be corrected, handles these moments differently. He looks first at himself. He searches for the truth in what others say and finds ways to adapt, change, and grow. Rather than being defensive toward others, he is on offense against the sin that lies within his own heart. The man who learns to do this becomes very wise and grows faster than others. Be that type of man today.

ASK THIS

From whom in your life do you need to get better at receiving correction?

DO THIS

Next time, receive their correction, worry less about items one through three above, say, "Thank you," and change.

PRAY THIS

God, give me direction and correction. Give me a chance to improve and become wise through the correction of others.

JOURNAL

TWO TYPES OF MEN

A WISDOM CHECKLIST

"A wise son makes a glad father,
but a foolish son is a sorrow to his mother."

Proverbs 10:1

I believe chapters 1 through 9 of Proverbs are the critical introduction that establishes the characteristics of a wise son, and then I see a progressive shift take place starting in chapter 10.

Let me illustrate. If you read Proverbs 10:1 without reading the nine chapters of introduction, you might assume that a good son makes a father glad. This is true, but it's only partially true. Yes, a good son makes a father happy. But Solomon is prequalifying this son. He calls him a *wise* son. Therefore, it's not just any son or a good son that makes a father glad. It's a wise son that makes a father glad.

Now we need to know what a wise son is like. The previous nine chapters identify seven features of a wise son (they apply to daughters too, by the way):

1. He fears the Lord.
2. He honors his parents.

3. He is responsible.

4. He works hard.

5. He treats people with respect.

6. He makes good friends.

7. He accepts correction.

What kind of son makes a father happy? A wise son with those seven qualities.

But this is a list of qualifiers not just for a wise son (or daughter). They are qualifiers for a wise father too. You see, Solomon assumes that a wise son also has a wise father. And since I assume you are a son and perhaps also a father, you now have a nice list of qualities or attributes to aim for in your life. A wisdom checklist.

It's a wise son that makes a father glad.

Note that it's not a *righteousness* checklist. Jesus checked that list off for us. This is a list of qualities to strive for as we grow in wisdom.

So grow in wisdom today. But since a list like this might be a little overwhelming, identify one item on it that you might need to work on—just one of these seven. And then I want you to take a moment to ask God to give you guidance in this area. Then pick another tomorrow, and the next one on the next day, and so on. Let's grow in wisdom together.

ASK THIS

Which one on the list of seven do you need to address today?

DO THIS

Ask God for an opportunity to grow in this area.

PRAY THIS

God, hear my request and make me a little wiser today.

JOURNAL

A WISDOM CHECKLIST

WHEN THE WAR RAGES

"With his mouth the godless man would destroy his
neighbor, but by knowledge the righteous are delivered.
When it goes well with the righteous, the city rejoices,
and when the wicked perish there are shouts of gladness."

Proverbs 11:9–10

These verses describe the tension of our time so well. Some people try to cancel and de-platform those with whom they disagree. In our politically divided culture, both sides use their platforms to bully people, destroying their credibility and gain. Yet at the same time, and also on both sides, a counterforce is working against that destruction. It is the knowledge of the righteous man who works to deliver those who have been destroyed. And what arises is a groundswell of cheer when these strongholds of unrighteousness and untruth are overthrown.

But I want you to see beyond the tension and to the wisdom of Solomon in his description of the righteous man's response. It's subtle. Solomon asserts that in the middle of the tension, righteous men should do the following:

1. Act neighborly.
2. Speak thoughtfully.

3. Think in godly ways.

4. Live righteously.

5. Rejoice always.

_______ A groundswell of cheer arises when strongholds of unrighteousness and untruth are overthrown. _______

The real challenge for us as men is consciously doing these things in the middle of the raging war in our lives today. So, get out there and try it. This is your battle: to act neighborly, speak thoughtfully, think in godly ways, live righteously, and rejoice always.

ASK THIS

Which of the five things do you need to act on immediately?

DO THIS

Don't hesitate; do it immediately.

PRAY THIS

God, help me to act neighborly, speak thoughtfully, think in godly ways, live righteously, and rejoice always.

JOURNAL
WHEN THE WAR RAGES

THE UNSAFE ADVENTURE

"Where there is no guidance, a people falls, but in an
abundance of counselors there is safety."

Proverbs 11:14

Men are fascinating creatures, aren't we? We love adventure. I know I do.
It is why I live the way I do. But in my search for adventure, I sometimes
detach the rudder. I sail out into the wide-open sea without guidance,
looking for a "pure" experience. I have done this many times in my career,
relationships, finances, and more. It sounds heroic, but it leads to catastrophic failure.

And it's not a fall that affects only us; it affects others as well.
Notice Solomon says that a *people* will fall. It's a decision by one that
affects many.

On the other hand, when a man obtains wise counsel, something
changes. Solomon says, "There is safety." Maybe that sounds boring, but
safety is not non-adventure. Safety is an adventure with fewer fails.
Safety is an adventure with other adventurous men. Safety is an adventure with counsel that avoids the stupidity of a lone man who says, "I
don't need guidance."

> Safety is not non-adventure. Safety is an adventure with fewer fails.

The lesson is this: if you want more adventure, find adventurous men and bring them along. Do it—get counsel. Before you make that next big decision, meet with someone who can give you godly advice. Don't sail the open sea alone. That's stupid, not safe. Live in the adventure, and do it with other adventurous men. This way, you will experience a bigger and better adventure, with new limits, at faster speeds, and with men who help keep the rudder attached.

ASK THIS

What kind of godly counsel do you need right now?

Who is someone who might have this wisdom?

DO THIS

Be adventurous and set a meeting with him.

PRAY THIS

God, give me godly counsel through the right godly man.

JOURNAL
THE UNSAFE ADVENTURE

AVOID STUPIDITY

"Whoever loves discipline loves knowledge,
but he who hates reproof is stupid."

Proverbs 12:1

This is such a simple proverb, and yet it contains so much wisdom. But the irony in the proverb is that stupid men won't get it. Mainly because they will resist being rebuked about their stupidity. Because to gain wisdom and grow in knowledge, you must love one thing that some men don't love: discipline.

Most men don't love discipline because they cannot get beyond the pain of the discipline to the knowledge contained within it. They get physically stumped or emotionally hijacked by the pain and never experience the joy of living on the other side.

Learn the lesson of the reproof and love it.

When you experience correction, just receive it. Stop resisting it. Receive it and gain knowledge. Learn the lesson of the reproof and love it. But love the knowledge you gained even more than the discipline itself. This will help us break the cycle of our stupidity.

ASK THIS

What's the discipline you need to stop resisting or the knowledge the discipline is trying to teach you?

DO THIS

Accept the discipline and love the knowledge.

PRAY THIS

God, I accept the discipline. You are the teacher, and I am the student.

ESCAPE THE SNARE

"An evil man is ensnared by the transgression of his lips,
but the righteous escapes from trouble."

Proverbs 12:13

It's possible to read Proverbs and conclude that righteous men will never suffer. But in this verse, we see this is not the case. Both evil men and righteous men experience trouble. The difference is how they experience it. The evil man brings it on himself and gets trapped by it. The righteous man has it brought upon him, but he escapes the snare.

The difference between the two men is twofold as well. First, there is a contrast in the integrity of each man's words. Second, there is a contrast in the type of man each one is: evil versus righteous. And thus, we learn that the words a man speaks reveal a lot about who he is—and vice versa.

> The words a man speaks
> reveal a lot about who
> he is—and vice versa.

So today, consider removing a word from your language. Remove an empty and useless word that does not strengthen your integrity. One that has ensnared you and might be ensnaring others. Delete it from your vocabulary and let it be a sacrifice to the Lord. Speak carefully, live with integrity, and escape the snare of the evil man.

ASK THIS

What word (or words) do you need to delete from your language to increase your integrity?

DO THIS

Leave the word(s) behind.

PRAY THIS

God, change me and the words I speak as a righteous man.

JOURNAL
ESCAPE THE SNARE

PERFECT SATISFACTION

"The righteous has enough to satisfy his appetite,
but the belly of the wicked suffers want."

Proverbs 13:25

There is something about gastrointestinal bliss, isn't there? Where your belly feels just right after that perfect meal so that the body is delighted with the ideal post-meal contentment. But Solomon is not talking only about the feeling of food in the stomach. He's also alluding to the unseen contentment within the righteous man's soul.

Brother, the righteous man lives with incredible soul satisfaction. This is because he knows that satisfaction comes only from God. This man doesn't fret about the things of this life, because his soul is always full. In those times when he may have less, in external terms, he still finds his satisfaction in God. And in those times when he has more, he also finds his satisfaction in God. He is trained by godly satisfaction to be content whatever the circumstance.

Contentment is not about what you have or don't have—it's about who you know. And we know a God who has all things. He satisfies. So find satisfaction in him and be content today.

Contentment is not about what you have or don't have—it's about who you know.

ASK THIS

Where in your life do you need to learn contentment? Do you need to find satisfaction in God when you have less or more?

DO THIS

Learn to be content by finding satisfaction in God.

PRAY THIS

God, thank you for satisfying my soul. You are enough.

JOURNAL
PERFECT SATISFACTION

JUST WALK AWAY

"Leave the presence of a fool, for there you
do not meet words of knowledge."

Proverbs 14:7

I love proverbs that are practical and easy to apply, because sometimes we need to be told what to do. And this one does that.

How many times have you been in a group conversation that took a sudden turn toward topics that were less than glorifying to God? These moments catch me by surprise. Often, they become suddenly disgusting, despicable, or derogatory. But the wisdom of this proverb is simple: we don't need to come up with something to say; we just need to walk away. That's it.

Sometimes we don't have to say anything to speak up for what is right and righteous. All we need to do is change our physical proximity to the conversation. Others often immediately understand when we turn our backs to them.

—— This proverb's wisdom is simple: we don't need to come up with something to say; we just need to walk away. ——

The next time you encounter this situation, I want you just politely and graciously to walk away. Don't say a word.

If you find you have too many people in your life who say foolish things, then maybe it's time to rethink your connections, community, or even the company you work for. Just something for you to ponder today. Could it be time to take a longer season away?

ASK THIS

What conversations do you anticipate that you might have to walk away from today?

DO THIS

Just walk away.

PRAY THIS

God, give me the awareness and courage to walk away today.

JOURNAL
JUST WALK AWAY

WORDS HAVE POWER

"A gentle tongue is a tree of life,
but perverseness in it breaks the spirit."

Proverbs 15:4

This verse makes me think of every man—be it a boss, coach, or friend—who has spoken harsh words to me. Though I cannot recall many of the exact things they said, I can remember the crushing experience of hearing the harsh words they spoke.

The very next thought I have after reading this verse is about all the harsh words *I* have spoken. Words that have broken the spirits of my wife, kids, employees, and friends.

Yet there is hope in this proverb. It offers a different approach and manner of speaking. One that is not perverse. It is a soft and gentle redirection that promotes life. It results in growth, budding, and fruitfulness in those who hear it. Instead of destroying someone, it guides them to become more.

This is what wise men know how to do. They know how to use words to guide others to become more than they are at present. Sometimes this is a word of redirection spoken gently. Sometimes it is a word of encouragement that promotes continued growth.

I challenge you to speak gentle words of redirection. When allowed to correct another person, instead of being harsh, hateful, and hurtful, take a new approach. Pause for a second or two and catch yourself in that heated moment. Then take a deep breath and hold your tongue. When your heart, mind, and mouth are ready, give correction—but do it ever so gently. And then pray that your redirection will take hold deeper within the person's heart.

> When allowed to correct another person, instead of being harsh, hateful, and hurtful, speak gentle words of redirection.

Don't become a bad memory of a harsh word spoken to people you love. Be a wise man, lead better, and guide people with gentler words.

ASK THIS

Who in your life needs gentle correction?

DO THIS

Speak and lead with words gently spoken.

PRAY THIS

God, convict me when I am harsh. Give me a gentler approach. Use me to speak carefully to others.

JOURNAL
WORDS HAVE POWER

THE COMMITTED AND ESTABLISHED MAN

Sometimes we act as if this verse says, "Make plans, get to work, and then ask God to establish them." But the flaw in this is the assumption that we can make perfect plans that need just a sprinkle of blessing from the Lord. This is an arrogant assumption. I highly recommend not doing this, as God might teach you an unfortunate lesson.

Besides, this is not what the proverb is teaching us. The first word of this proverb assumes the first action is *committing*. The man who is committed to the Lord works for the Lord. He knows what God wants him to work on. He will discern the difference between God's work and his work. And when he does God's work, he will do it only God's way. Thus, this man's plan is adjusted to God's will and becomes God's plan. And while it may look like to the world that this man's plan is being established, it is really God's plan that is being established in and through an already committed man.

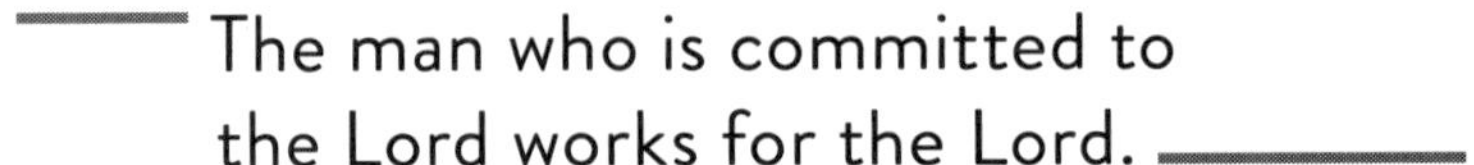

The man who is committed to the Lord works for the Lord.

To waste less time working on the wrong thing, spend a few minutes praying about your commitment to God and not his commitment to your plans.

ASK THIS

Do you need direction today?

DO THIS

Be committed to God and committed to his plan done his way.

PRAY THIS

God, I need your direction. I commit myself to you. I want your plans to be my plans so that your will is established through me.

JOURNAL

THE COMMITTED AND ESTABLISHED MAN

COMMANDING NEXT STEPS

"The heart of man plans his way,
but the LORD establishes his steps."

Proverbs 16:9

As men, we should dream, cast vision, develop strategies, and tend to our financial investments. But godly men never forget that there is one who has tactical command of all things. He has command over all creation and even the steps we take on the way through life. He is our Lord. And he's ultimately going to decide the next steps in the plan.

But this fact shouldn't quench our passion or our planning. It just means we should be willing to let go of our passion and planning when God has something different in mind. He is our Lord and the one who establishes our steps. And the Lord regulates this to remind us that he is always in control and will always have better plans than we could ever contrive. It's the way he trains us to give glory to him, rather than stealing it for ourselves on those days when we think our plans are so great.

> The Lord is always in control and
> will always have better plans than
> we could ever contrive.

There are two potential practical responses to this proverb. First, if you are feeling a little confused about your next steps, then ask God to establish those steps. And when he does, give him all the credit. Second, if you tend to feel a little overconfident in the plans you make, then ask God to clarify his plan. I would do this before you get tripped up with some unexpected bumps God puts in your path.

ASK THIS

Are you feeling confused or overconfident today?

DO THIS

Bring your plans to God.

PRAY THIS

God, show me the way and the next steps I need to take.

JOURNAL
COMMANDING NEXT STEPS

ARE YOU A FRIEND OR BROTHER?

"A friend loves at all times,
and a brother is born for adversity."

Proverbs 17:17

This proverb gives next-level meaning to the nouns *friend* and *brother*. The word *friend* represents one level of a relationship we can have with another man, while *brother* refers to a relationship that is the next level up. A brother is there for us during and through the adversity. He is someone who will hang with us during those hard times.

We need friends, but we also need brothers. Brothers are men who will stand by our side when we face adverse moments. They won't wrestle against us but with us through the challenges we face. These men are much more than friends. That's why we give them the title *brother*.

A brother is there for us during
and through the adversity.

If you don't have a brother, get one. Because guess what: adversity is coming. And friends are nice, but brothers are way better.

ASK THIS

Who is your brother?

DO THIS

Send him a text and tell him thanks for being a brother.

PRAY THIS

God, give me brothers for my time of adversity.

JOURNAL

ARE YOU A FRIEND OR BROTHER?

EVERYONE HAS AN OPINION

"A fool takes no pleasure in understanding, but only in
expressing his opinion…. A fool's lips walk into a fight,
and his mouth invites a beating. A fool's mouth is his
ruin, and his lips are a snare to his soul."

Proverbs 18:2, 6–7

Wow! These words cut like a scalpel, don't they? This is a direct address to the propagandists of our time.

Notice the double trouble in the first sentence. The writer imagines a man whom he calls "a fool." He then states two traits about him that confirm he is a fool: First, he has no desire to understand. Second, he continues to voice his opinion.

If you reflect on the combination of these two traits and look at how our society has evolved, you will discover many who behave like this. You will see it all around you—men and women on both ends of the political spectrum who have no desire to understand yet have unrelenting opinions.

The results of this behavior are catastrophic. In the second two verses, we are told what happens to someone who acts this way: their mouth invites a conflict. Just take note of the conflicts around you today.

See if it doesn't stem from fools expressing their opinions but lacking understanding.

But the conflict is not just one of words. It comes from a conflict within the soul. They may be unaware of it, but such a person's soul is in turmoil. Their understanding is clouded, and yet they still open their mouth.

The sad truth is that we have all been this man. We have opened our mouths without understanding, thus inflicting harm on another. But the issue is not just with our minds and mouths. The issue stems from our souls.

> When we inflict harm on others with what we say, often the issue is not just with our minds and mouths. The issue stems from our souls.

Before you open your mouth today, make sure your soul is set on God. Before you open your cakehole, invite the Spirit to give your soul a prompting and your mind understanding. And then speak. If you are not sure your soul is set or that you are ready to speak, remember this acronym: KMS (keep mouth shut).

> Even a fool who keeps silent is considered wise; when he closes his lips, he is deemed intelligent. (Prov. 17:28)

ASK THIS

Is your soul set on the Lord?

DO THIS

Speak when your soul is ready; otherwise, KMS.

PRAY THIS

God, may every word that comes from my mouth and the meditation of my heart be from and of you.

JOURNAL
EVERYONE HAS AN OPINION

DISCOVER VISION

One thing that captures me about a man is his vision: the vision he has for life, future, career, and family. Over the years, though, I have discovered that much of a man's vision is a futile attempt to play God.

I may have a good idea of what I want to do, but then God has his plan. And sometimes, his plan competes with my plan. In that case, there is only one winner. And it ain't me.

Unfortunately, it has taken me a lot of years to figure this one out.

For example, in 2014, I founded the ministry I lead today: Resolute. At the time, I thought I had a pretty good idea about how it should look and what we were going to do. I wrote a fifty-plus-page business plan full of vision, goals, strategies, and tactics. I thought I knew the right things to do. But over the years, I have flipped back through that document, only to discover that everything in it is different from what we actually ended up doing.

We can cast all the vision we want, but it is God who orders a man's steps. It's God who decides how things will work from one day to the next.

This is why I wince today when I hear a man, pastor, or leader cast a vision. Because they can have great goals and dreams, and they can even stir passion in masses of people. But if it ain't God's vision, it ain't gonna work. No man gets to play God. Only the Lord orders a man's steps.

Now, while it's impossible to cast a vision of the future that will come about with 100 percent accuracy, I have discovered that I can take steps of obedience every day. And that's what I have done since this ministry began. It has not followed a clear business plan, but I don't think God cares. What God wants is obedience from me.

Here's the amazing part: I have found that when you are obedient one day, then the next, and the next over a long period of time, you will usually be able to look back and realize the vision God has for you. You will finally see and discover the path he has you on. And then you will see not your vision but his.

> Our ministry has not followed a clear business plan, but I don't think God cares. What God wants is obedience from me.

When you do catch a glimpse of this vision, don't go out and tell other people that this was your vision. It was never yours. It was God's. He just revealed it to you over time and in a way that you could handle it and stay humble at the same time.

He is the God of all vision, and you are always just a mere mortal man. When you get to this point in your journey, you will understand a bit of the mysterious ways of the Lord our God.

Let him lead today. Stop worrying about your vision. Just be obedient to him one day at a time.

ASK THIS

Where is your vision getting in the way of God's?

DO THIS

Take one step of obedience today.

PRAY THIS

Father, may I always be obedient. Reveal your ways to me.

JOURNAL
DISCOVER VISION

FIGHT THE BATTLE

"The horse is made ready for the day of battle,
but the victory belongs to the LORD."

Proverbs 21:31

In this text, we are introduced to battle imagery. I'm sure Solomon was imagining real-life hand-to-hand combat on a field of war, but there are all kinds of battles.

Physical battles are rare for us, but spiritual battles are not. We fight them every day. Today, you are going to fight them. One day, it's a battle for our marriage. The next day, it is a battle for our children. The next, we get attacked at work for our beliefs and values. The next is some private battle with sin. And on the worst of days, it's a battle with all of them at the same time.

Most of these battles are unseen—known only to us. Yet we must prepare. As Solomon says, we must make ready. We must prepare our horses, ready our armor, sharpen the sword, and set the battle plan.

But here's the deal: we may prepare, but God is the one who gains the victory. We must keep this at the forefront of our minds. If we take the battle into our own hands, we might get in the way of the God who fights for us.

Does this mean we should prepare less? No. Does this mean we should not fight when the time is right? No. Does this mean we should not be passionate in the battle? No. What it means is that when we prepare for battle, run to battle, and fight the battle, we fight as a representative of the Lord, who is going to win, and the victory is his, so we better make sure we fight his way.

> We may prepare, but God is the one who gains the victory. We must keep this at the forefront of our minds.

So get ready. Prepare! Because a battle is coming today. And it might be intense. Prepare, but let God lead. For when he leads, he wins. The victory is his—not yours.

ASK THIS

What battle will you meet today?

DO THIS

Prepare and let God lead.

PRAY THIS

Father, ready my resources. My mind. My heart. My soul. The battle is on. Be my victory.

JOURNAL
FIGHT THE BATTLE

THE EXTREME VALUE OF CHARACTER

"A good name is to be chosen rather than great riches,
and favor is better than silver or gold."

Proverbs 22:1

Draw your attention to the word "name" in the text today.

A name is something that identifies a person. Each of us is given a name at birth. We don't get a choice in the name we are given, because it is given to us before we know who we are. Yet as we get older, we start giving shape to our name based on our actions. Over time, other titles or labels attach themselves to our name. We act smart, so we become known as intelligent. We act jovial and thus become known as funny. As we continue to grow, our choices and actions shape us even more. They chisel out our character.

Thus, when we call a person by name, we instantly make a character connection. For example, think about what image comes to your mind when I say a well-known name like Winston Churchill. Or what comes to mind when you hear the name Lee Harvey Oswald? Or how about Jeffrey Epstein? You instantly associate certain events and character attributes with that person. They could be positive or negative attributes, and though people are a lot more complex than one or two attributes, it is how we define some people.

The same is true of us. When someone says your name, specific images come to their mind. Your name identifies you with character attributes derived from your actions. I think of character as the sum of all the decisions we make in this life, and this text accentuates that truth.

But it also teaches us that our name and its character have the potential to hold a higher value than some of the most valuable commodities in this life—like silver or gold.

So today, don't sell your value short. Make great choices and better decisions. Build character. Build extreme value. Pursue actions that are becoming of a godly man, and worry less about the world's riches. Riches of this life are temporary. They come and go, and so do their value. Invest in an appreciating asset: character. It's the best investment.

If you're like me and have made some poor choices that have impacted your character and name, you might need to hear this. In Christ, and only in him, can you cancel an old identity and discover a new one. Only Jesus can address a life of bad choices and decisions. And only in him will you find a new identity. Seek him. His name is one of extreme character and value, and he wants to give you a new name!

> Therefore, if anyone is in Christ, he is a new creation.
> The old has passed away; behold, the new has come.
> (2 Cor. 5:17)

Riches of this life come and go, and so do their value. Invest in an appreciating asset: character. It's the best investment.

ASK THIS

Have you made a decision that is negatively affecting your character?

DO THIS

Confess this to God and make new choices.

PRAY THIS

Father, forgive me, for I have sinned. I bring my life of bad decisions to you. Give me a new identity in Christ.

JOURNAL

A BIBLICAL POSITION ON DRINKING

"Who has woe? Who has sorrow? Who has strife?
Who has complaining? Who has wounds without cause?
Who has redness of eyes? Those who tarry long
over wine; those who go to try mixed wine."

Proverbs 23:29–30

This section is a warning about what happens to those who drink excessively. You may not know this, but the Bible has much to say about drinking.

For example, by chapter 9 of the first book of the Bible, we already have a story about someone who got drunk. It wasn't just anybody, either, but a significant figure in biblical history—Noah. After the flood, Noah, who was God's man, planted a vineyard and got hammered (Gen. 9:21).

A little further along in the Genesis story, a descendant of Noah, Lot, was given excessive amounts of wine by his two daughters, who deliberately got him drunk so they might have sex with him to preserve their lineage (Gen. 19:33–38). Throughout the Bible, you can find several stories about men who drank too much.

Yet the Bible doesn't restrict drinking—it restricts *drunkenness*. If you are self-controlled enough to drink in moderation, drinking is fine. Even Jesus drank wine (Matt. 11:18–19), and his very first miracle was to provide more wine for a wedding (John 2:1–11). Yet there are other men in the Bible, like John the Baptist, who never drank. Therefore, both moderation and abstinence are acceptable positions on drinking, according to the Bible.

But in this text, Solomon helps us see six effects of excessive drinking, which he poses in questions. In the first set of questions, he alludes to emotional problems of the drunkard: woe and sorrow. In the second set of questions, he refers to social problems of the drunkard: strife and complaining. And in the third set of questions, he identifies physical problems of the drunkard: wounds and redness of the eyes.

Doesn't that list pretty much describe the people in every dive bar we have seen? Seated at bars across the world are men with emotional, social, and physical problems. But there is no solution for any of those problems to be found in drinking. It is true that excessive drinking might help you forget your problems for a short time. But when the intoxication wears off, your problems will be waiting, and you might discover you have developed a new problem: an addiction.

If this is the case for you today, there is a solution. The answer begins with a spiritual step. I know this doesn't sound intuitive, because we think to address the drinking problem, we need to focus on the drinking problem. And yes, drinking is a problem that needs attention, but it's only a symptom of the problem—a problem with you. Real change to who you are does not begin with what you do. It starts with who you are.

Drinking may have been your attempt to solve a much bigger problem with you. The Bible teaches that we are spiritual people who need spiritual solutions. It teaches that the only solution is the power of Christ living in us. It is only by the spiritual power given to us by Christ that we will find victory over our drinking problems that have masked every other problem—emotional, social, and physical.

Real change to who you are
does not begin with what you do.
It starts with who you are.

You can try to stop drinking, but this is futile. Your own strength is not enough. You need divine power. Because this power gives supernatural victory in every daily battle against those problems that can change desires and behaviors.

I have been crucified with Christ. It is no longer I who live, but Christ who lives in me. And the life I now live in the flesh I live by faith in the Son of God, who loved me and gave himself for me.... But I say, walk by the Spirit, and you will not gratify the desires of the flesh. (Gal. 2:20; 5:16)

ASK THIS

Do you need spiritual power?

DO THIS

Become a new man—God's man—today and receive power.

PRAY THIS

God, I want to become a new man. Give me spiritual power to overcome all compulsions and addictions in my personal life.

JOURNAL

A BIBLICAL POSITION ON DRINKING

THE SWEET TASTE OF WISDOM

"My son, eat honey, for it is good, and the drippings of
the honeycomb are sweet to your taste. Know that
wisdom is such to your soul; if you find it, there will be
a future, and your hope will not be cut off."

Proverbs 24:13–14

I love this one because Solomon includes details of taste, which add a tangible lesson to this proverb. The command is for his son to eat honey. As we know, honey is full of sugar. And sugar fires the taste-receptor cells on the tip of the tongue, delivering a sugar high. It is so potent that energy is delivered directly to our bodies. We instantly feel this energy because sugar burns quickly in the human body.

But there is another reason he wants his son to eat honey. It's not just to get a sugar high. Solomon is hoping that as his son eats honey, he will be reminded of how wisdom works. Because wisdom works similarly. It delivers potent energy directly to the soul. Wisdom is an "eye-opening" experience. Sometimes it's so eye-opening that it allows a man to see into the future and therefore see his hope in times of hopelessness.

_______ Wisdom delivers potent energy
directly to the soul. _______

The application is this: When you feel hopeless, get a little honey. Eat it and be reminded that wisdom works the same way. It is sweetness for the soul that opens your eyes to the future and delivers the energy to hope again.

ASK THIS

Do you need hope today?

DO THIS

Get wisdom.

PRAY THIS

God, today I need hope. I am asking you for wisdom. I am ready to receive it regardless of how you present it. Help me pay attention today when it comes, and give me hope.

JOURNAL

THE SWEET TASTE OF WISDOM

BROTHERS MAKE US SHARPER

"Iron sharpens iron, and one man sharpens another."

Proverbs 27:17

The image here is epic. Imagine the workshop of a master-level ironsmith. You see him walk over to a large wooden barrel from which he selects a raw piece of iron. He surveys it in his hands, envisioning what it might become. Next, he gives it shape by heating and striking it. One hard swing after another, his sledge draws the iron out. And here, for the first time, we notice a hint of what the iron is becoming.

But he's not finished. He sets down the sledge and exchanges it for a more aggressive tool—the grinder. He applies the iron to the spinning wheel, and sparks fly. With every turn, small pieces of iron are removed. As he continues, dullness is stripped away in his hands. The iron shines brighter and gets sharper.

This is the image Solomon uses to describe the value that one God-fearing man brings to another. With the help of a more experienced man, another man is made better. It takes a more experienced man to cast a vision for, shape, and sharpen other men. Without this a man tends toward uselessness, like a piece of raw iron sitting in a wooden barrel. And unused iron sitting in a barrel does only one thing—it rusts. But a man molded by the hands of a mentor or coach takes shape, is sharpened, and becomes useful.

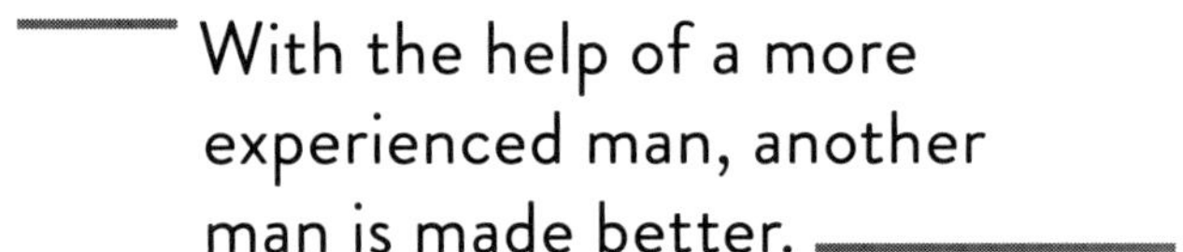

So, stop waiting. It's time to get sharper. Build a relationship with a man who has more experience than you do. Don't overcomplicate it. Just find someone who is great at something you are not and ask him just one question: "How do you do that?" And then heed any good and godly advice given to you.

ASK THIS

Who is one man more experienced than you who could give you insightful wisdom?

DO THIS

Ask that man for the guidance you need: "How do you do that?"

PRAY THIS

God, put wiser and more godly men in my path. I want to be a sharper man.

JOURNAL

BROTHERS MAKE US SHARPER

THE THINGS MEN PRAISE EXPOSE THEIR CHARACTER

"The crucible is for silver, and the furnace is for gold,
and a man is tested by his praise."

Proverbs 27:21

This one is simple, but it could sting a little. Here's why: a crucible and a furnace are fiery containers in which objects are refined and made more valuable. They are places where value is discovered.

For men, our praise is our crucible and our furnace. Our praise exposes us. The stuff we talk about the most determines what we value the most. If you talk most about recreation, then you value recreation. If it's your career you talk about the most, then you value your career. If it's your kids you talk most about, then you value your kids. Pretty simple.

> The stuff we talk about
> the most determines what
> we value the most.

The question I have for you today is this: How much do you talk about God?

Stings, right?

Try praising God a little more today. Start by praising him in prayer, and then praise him before others. Do the same tomorrow, and the next day and the next. Here's why we should: He is valuable. He is real value. And our praise should proclaim this all day long, so others can see his value through us.

ASK THIS

What is one thing you value about God?

DO THIS

Shout out a praise to God.

PRAY THIS

God, may I spend more time praising you and less time praising myself in what I am thinking about and talking about.

JOURNAL

THE THINGS MEN PRAISE EXPOSE THEIR CHARACTER

IT'S TIME TO GIVE A REBUKE

"Whoever rebukes a man will afterward find more favor
than he who flatters with his tongue."

Proverbs 28:23

Several times in my life, I have been rebuked or have had to rebuke another man. It's always uncomfortable, no matter which side you are on. Receiving a rebuke is hard. Delivering it is hard.

One thing I have learned from being on both sides of the experience is that a rebuke needs to have a benefit. So when we speak it, we should deliver it for the benefit of the other person. And when we receive it, we should look for the benefit. If both parties do this, a rebuke can be well delivered and well received.

Sadly, it rarely happens this way. That's because a rebuke involves a lot of emotion, both in how it's delivered and in how it's received. But there is a way to move through and beyond all this emotion, and that's for both parties to focus on the benefit.

As we saw a couple of days ago, iron sharpens iron only when there is grinding. In this proverb, we have an example of the grind. Rebuke is the grind. Flattery is not.

> The way to move through and beyond all the emotion involved with a rebuke is for both parties to focus on the benefit.

So today, who is someone you need to rebuke?

You might have someone on your mind right now. A friend, relative, son, daughter, sister, brother, or maybe even a colleague at work. What are you waiting for? You might be their only means of ever getting better. But do it well and for their benefit.

And if you happen to be on the receiving end, then work through the emotions and find the benefit they are trying to give. When you're done, you both might discover you are better for it.

ASK THIS

Who is someone you need to rebuke today?

DO THIS

Do it well.

PRAY THIS

God, give me the courage to rebuke and to receive rebukes well.

JOURNAL

IT'S TIME TO GIVE A REBUKE

SPENDING EXPOSES A MAN

"He who loves wisdom makes his father glad,
but a companion of prostitutes squanders his
wealth. By justice a king builds up the land,
but he who exacts gifts tears it down."

Proverbs 29:3–4

These two sentences form a parallel. They talk about two men, a son and a ruler, who both waste wealth. How they misuse their money exposes their character, their lust, and their greed.

Lust and greed don't just show up in these mature forms overnight. They start small. When lust and greed are small, it's usually not much of an issue, because the impact isn't that great. We might even dismiss it if we see it. We think it's just a little lust here or a little greed there.

But the problem is that, over time, we get comfortable with these longings, and they train us. We begin to think and behave in ungodly ways. And they are never satisfied. Thus, our lust and greed must take from others, and they become victims of our ungodly character.

To undo this corrupt cycle, we must be retrained. We must learn to love two things: wisdom and justice. Wisdom retrains our character, and justice is wisdom applied.

So today, a first step might be assessing your lust and greed in how you spend money. Examine your bank accounts for a while. Consider the waste you see and what it's declaring about your lust and greed. And then make a cut—a cut for the purpose of your character. I promise the benefits are great. They make a father proud, and they build up the land.

> We must learn to love two
> things: wisdom and justice.
> Wisdom retrains our character,
> and justice is wisdom applied.

ASK THIS

What do your accounts say about your lust and greed?

DO THIS

Make a cut to address your lust and greed.

PRAY THIS

God, I need strength and courage to address my lust and greed. Show me today where I can address these sins before they become even bigger.

JOURNAL

SPENDING EXPOSES A MAN

JOURNAL

ADDITIONAL
LINED PAGES

BE RESOLUTE

Join **Be Resolute**, a men's ministry platform founded by author Vince Miller that provides Bible studies aimed at building better men.

Find encouragement and truth

Sign up for the men's daily devo and join thousands of men all over the world.

Invite Vince to speak at your event

Bring this dynamic and devoted author and speaker to mentor the men at your ministry conference, event, or men's retreat.

Learn more at
beresolute.org

youtube.com/@VinceLeeMiller

beresolute.org   facebook.com/vincentleemiller   Instagram: @vinceleemiller